Rural USA Landscapes Coloring Book

Collection of Nature Landscape Sketches, Hand Drawings For Adults - Watercolor Painters

Rachel Mintz

Images used under license from Shutterstock.com

Copyright © 2018 Palm Tree Publishing - All rights reserved.
No part of this publication may be reproduced, distributed, or transmitted in any form or by any means, including photocopying, recording, or other electronic or mechanical methods, without the prior written permission of the publisher, except in the case of brief quotations embodied in critical reviews and certain other noncommercial uses permitted by copyright law.

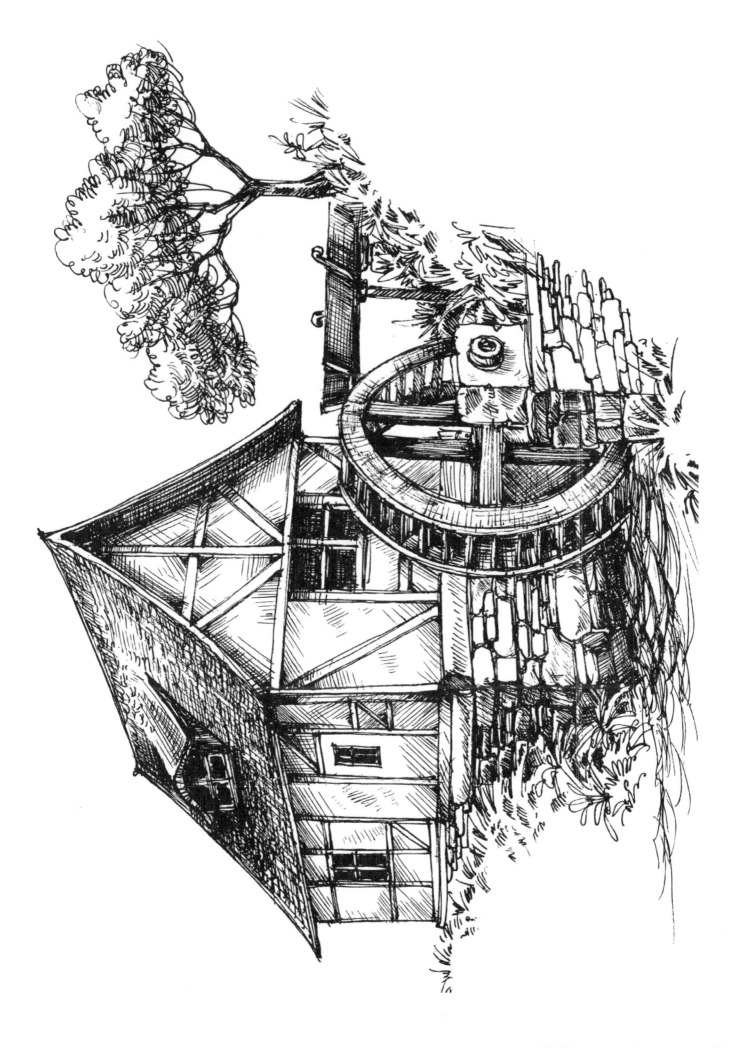

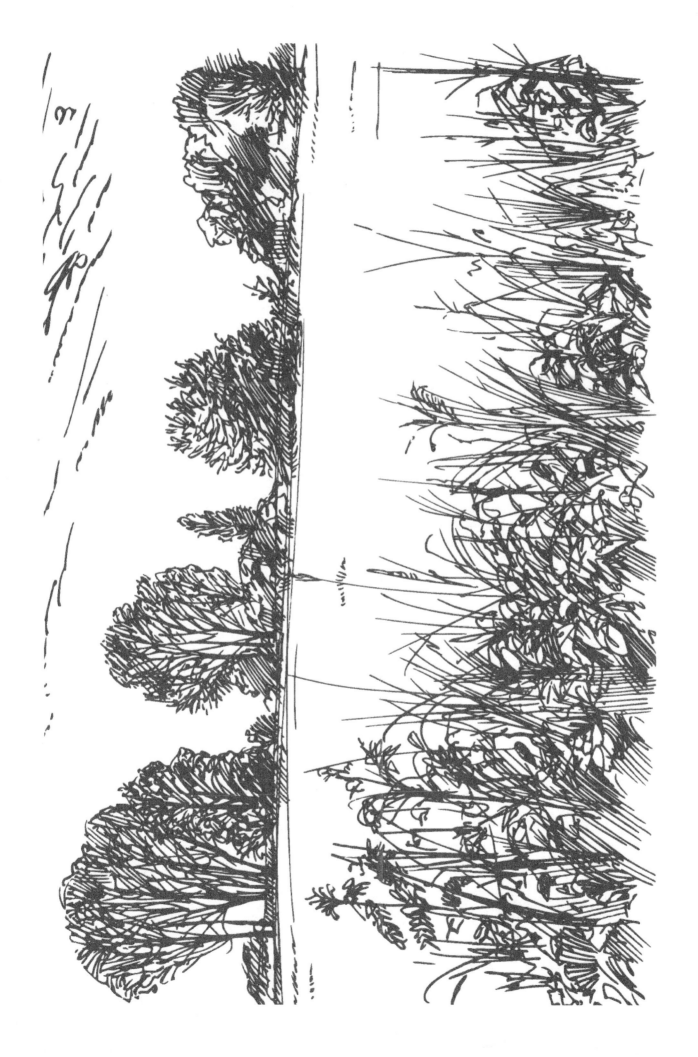

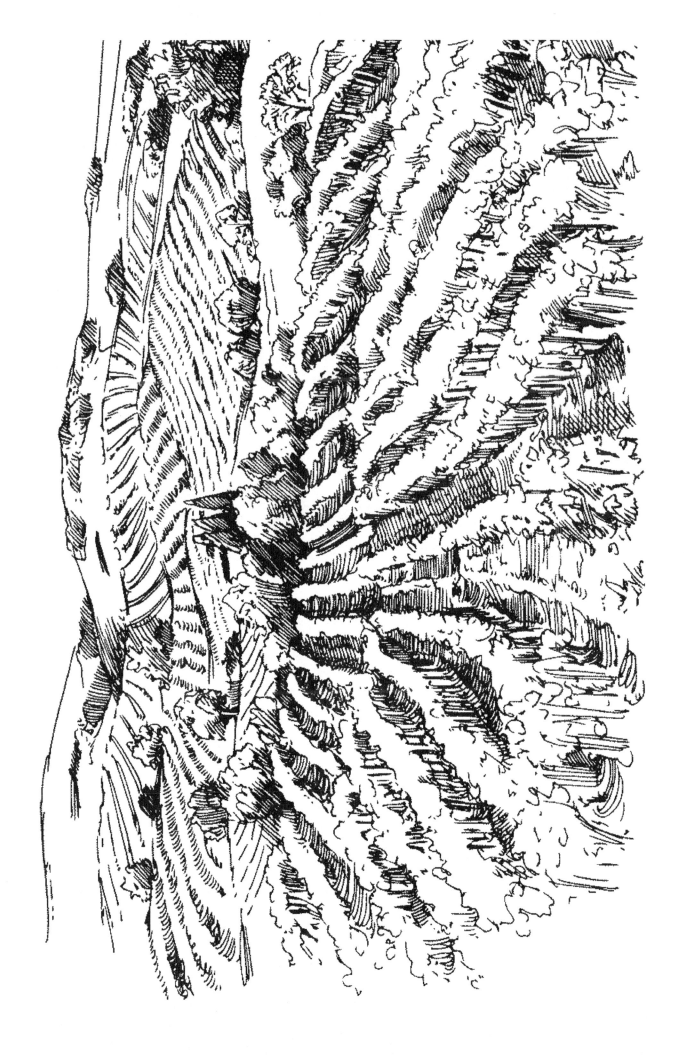

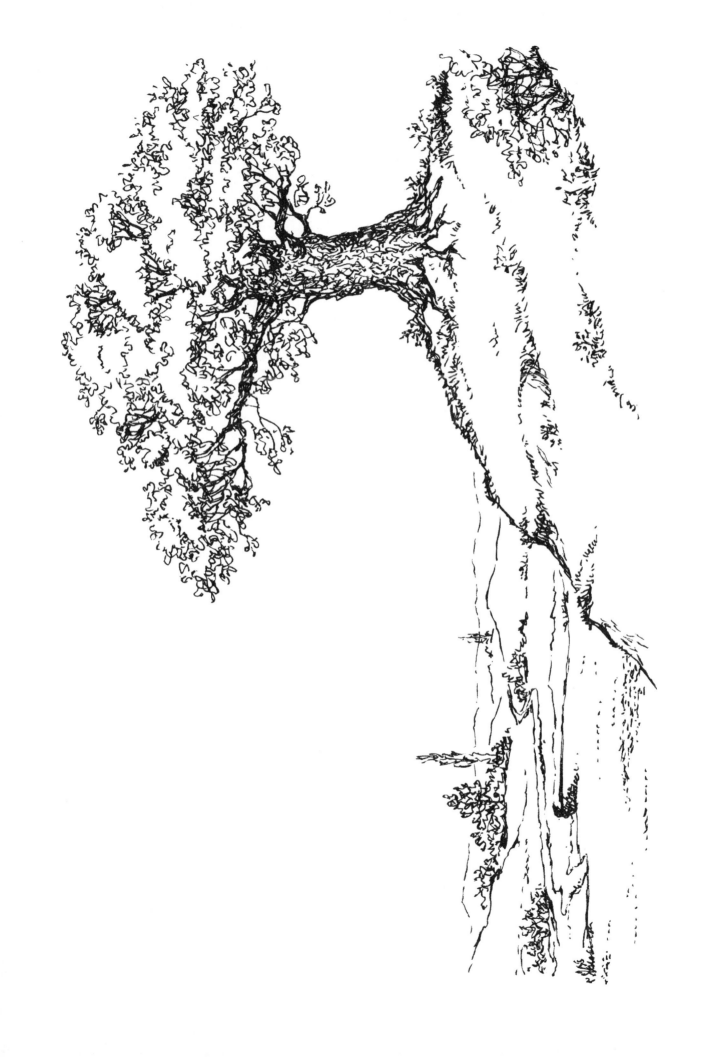

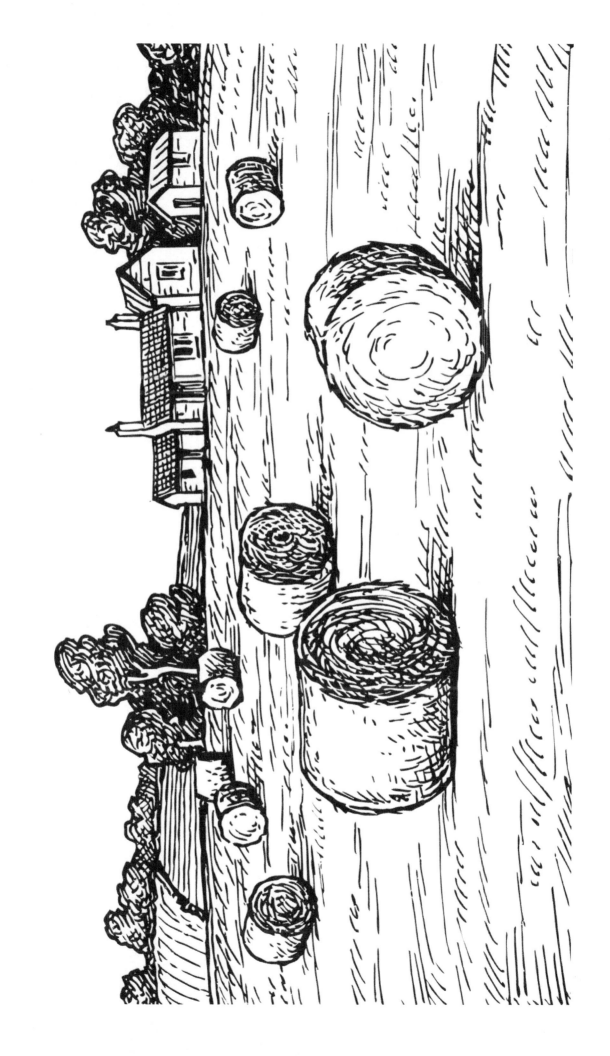

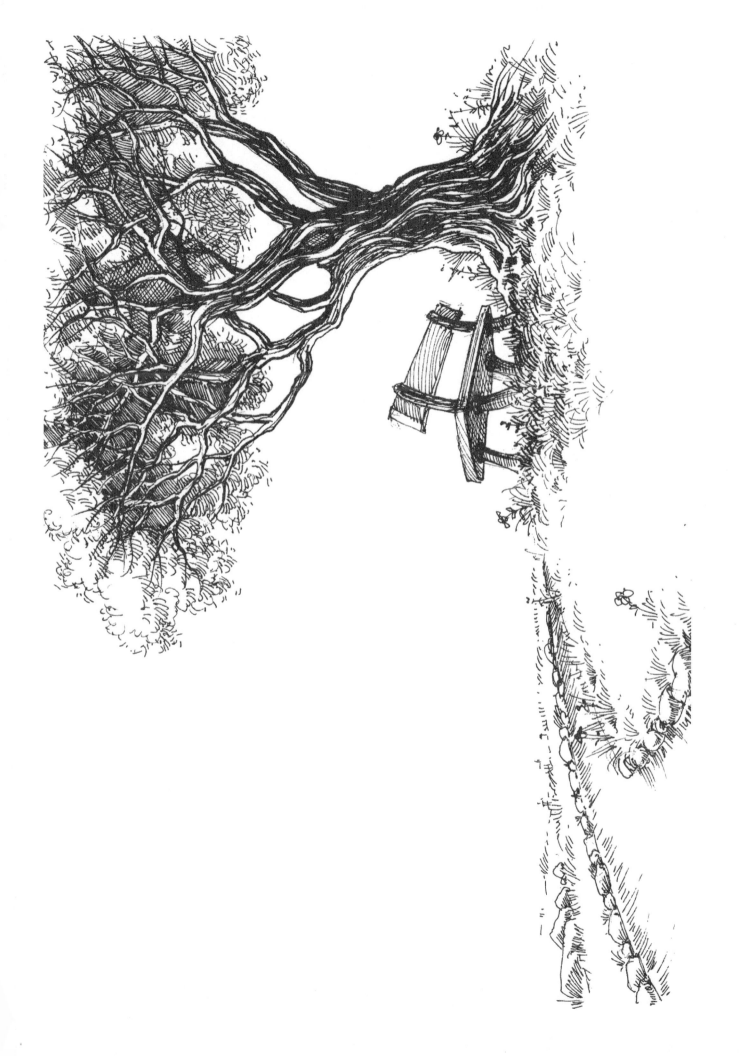

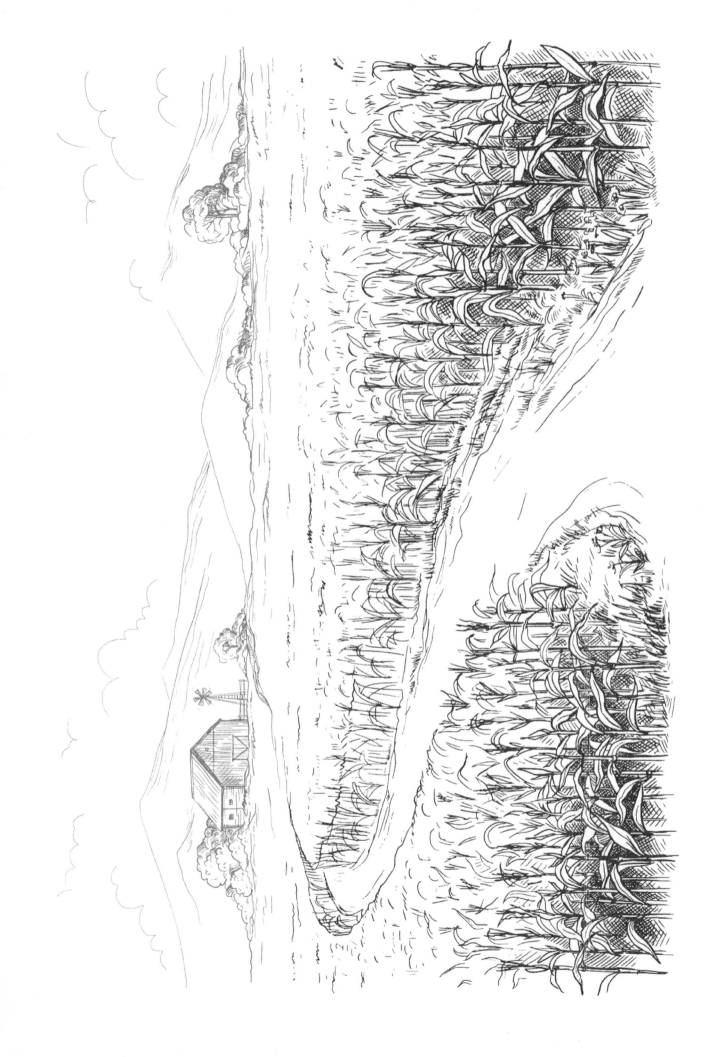

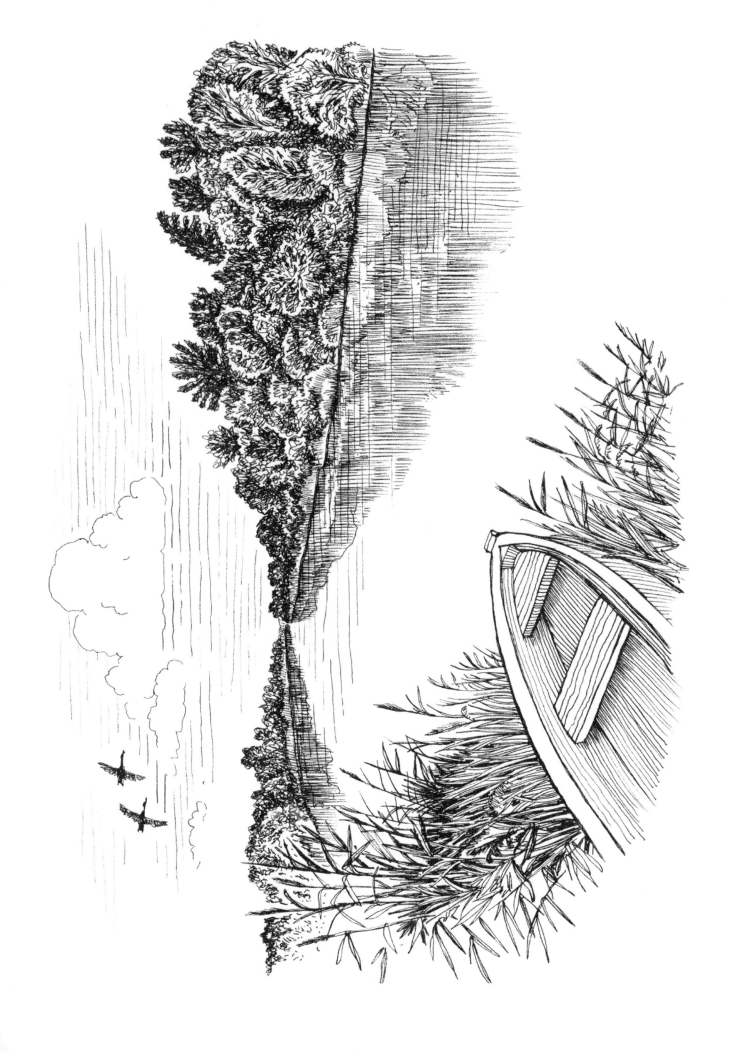

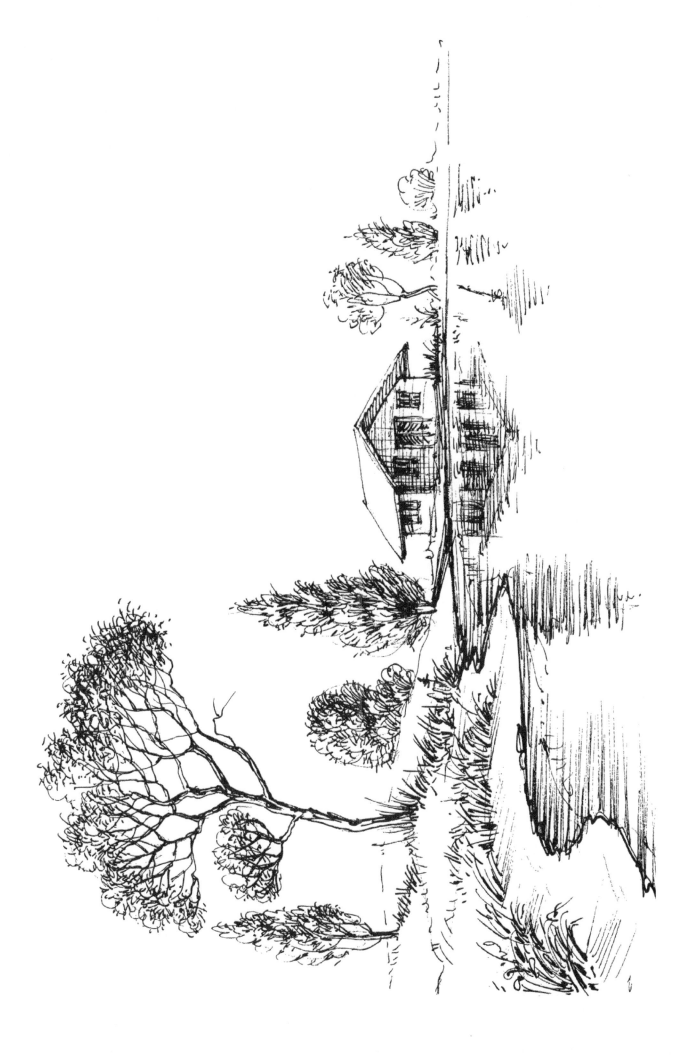

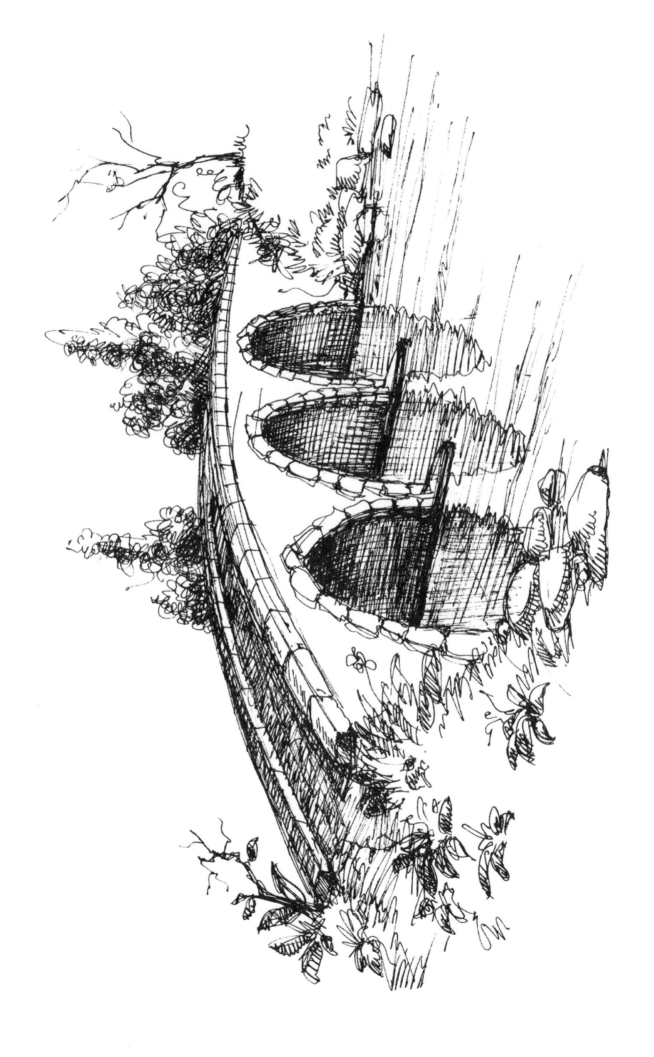

Thank you for coloring with us

Enjoy more from our coloring books catalogs:

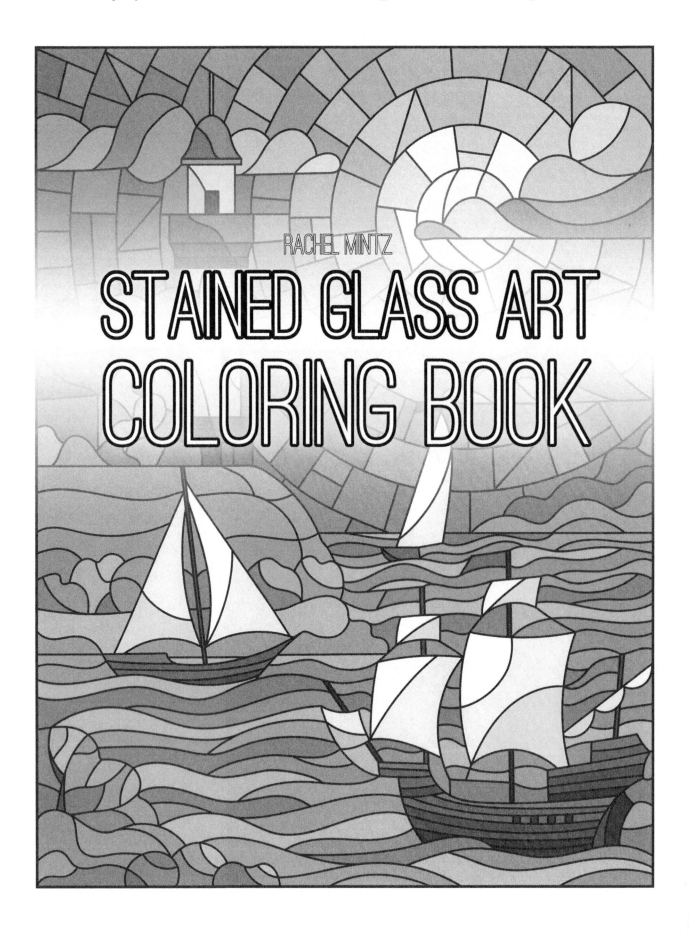

LUXURY BEDROOMS
COLORING BOOK FOR ADULTS

BEAUTIFUL LIGHTHOUSES
COLORING BOOK

RACHEL MINTZ

Thank you for coloring with us.

Printed in Great Britain
by Amazon